ADAM HAMILTON

D1617476

Forgiveness

Finding Peace Through Letting Go

Leader Guide

by John P. Gilbert

ABINGDON PRESS
NASHVILLE

FORGIVENESS:
FINDING PEACE THROUGH LETTING GO
LEADER GUIDE

This book is printed on elemental chlorine–free paper.
ISBN 978-1-5018-7068-2

18 19 20 21 22 23 24 25 26 27 — 10 9 8 7 6 5 4 3 2 1
MANUFACTURED IN THE UNITED STATES OF AMERICA

Contents

To the Group Leader

Welcome! In this study, you have an exciting opportunity to learn and grow with a group of Christians seeking to understand just what forgiveness is—and what it isn't.

You'll be leading the group, but always remember that you are also one of the learners. Your job is not to judge answers or grade responses but to facilitate the group's study and to engage in the learning process yourself.

The aim of the study is to explore the topic of forgiveness—in our relationship with God, with our spouses or romantic interests, with our parents and siblings, and with others in our lives. The four-session study is made up of several components:

- Adam Hamilton's book *Forgiveness: Finding Peace Through Letting Go;*
- a DVD in which Hamilton, using stories and Scripture, presents and expands upon key points from the book;
- this leader guide.

5

Using these components, you will lead the members of your group over the course of four sessions to examine the topic of forgiveness in the Bible and in our lives. For groups that would like a fifth session, this guide includes a list of discussion questions for the Epilogue.

Session Format

Because no two groups are alike, this guide has been designed to give you flexibility and choice in tailoring the sessions for your group. The session activities are listed below. You may choose any or all, adapting them as you wish to meet the schedule and needs of your particular group.

Getting Started
    Session Goals
    Opening Prayer
    Opening Activity

Learning Together
    Video Study and Discussion
    Book Study and Discussion
    Bible Study and Discussion

Wrapping Up
    Closing Activity
    Closing Prayer

Helpful Hints

Preparing for the Session

- Become familiar with the material before the group session. Read the book chapter and watch the video segment.

- Choose the session elements you will use during the group session, including the specific discussion questions you plan to cover.
- Secure a TV and DVD player in advance.
- Oversee room setup. Ideally, group members should be seated around a table or in a circle so that all can see each other. Moveable chairs are best, because the group will be breaking up into small teams.
- Bring a supply of Bibles for those who forget to bring their own. Having a variety of translations is helpful.
- Make paper and pens or pencils available at each session, and encourage group members to bring their own notepads.
- You will also need a chalkboard, a white board, or an easel with paper for each session.

Setting the Tone

- Begin and end on time.
- Be enthusiastic! Create a climate of participation, encouraging individuals to participate, as they feel comfortable.
- Communicate the importance of group discussions and group exercises.
- If no one answers at first during discussions, do not be afraid of a silence. Count silently to ten; then say something such as, "Would anyone like to go first?" If no one responds, venture an answer yourself and ask for comments.
- Model openness as you share with the group. Group members will follow your example. If you limit your sharing to a surface level, others will follow suit.
- Encourage multiple answers or responses before moving on.
- Ask, "Why?" or "Why do you believe that?" to help continue a discussion and give it greater depth.
- Affirm others' responses with comments such as "Great" or "Thanks" or "Good insight"—especially if this is the first time someone has spoken during the group session.

- Give everyone a chance to talk, but keep the conversation moving. Moderate to prevent a few individuals from doing all the talking.
- Monitor your own contributions. If you are doing most of the talking, back off so that you do not train the group to listen rather than speak up.
- Remember that you do not have all the answers. Your job is to keep the discussion going and encourage participation.

Managing the Session

- Honor the time schedule. If a session is running longer than expected, get consensus from the group before continuing beyond the agreed-upon ending time.
- Consider involving group members in various aspects of the group session, such as playing the DVD, saying prayers, or reading the Scripture.
- Understand that the subject of forgiveness may strike raw nerves with some of the group members. Be alert for this and do not press too hard if someone is showing signs of discomfort.
- Note that the session guides sometimes call for breaking into smaller teams. This gives everyone a chance to speak and participate fully. Mix up the teams; don't let the same people pair up on every activity.
- Because many activities call for personal sharing, confidentiality is essential. Group members should never pass along stories that have been shared in the group. Remind the group members at each session: confidentiality is crucial to the success of this study.
- You are the group leader. Prepare yourself with prayer as you begin your study of each chapter, as you ponder the learning activities in the leader guide, and as you prepare to lead. Then pray for each group member by name before each session. The Holy Spirit will lead and guide you.

1.

The Divine Answer

Getting Started

Session Goals

This session is intended to help participants

- reflect on God's forgiveness and what it means for us;
- discuss the meaning and application of forgiveness, sin, and repentance;
- focus on the burden involved in carrying unforgiven sin and on the process of letting that burden go;
- address and discuss issues related to understanding forgiveness with "head" comprehension—as contrasted with experiencing forgiveness in the heart and soul.

Opening Prayer

Begin this session, and all sessions, with a prayer for illumination. Recognize that the Holy Spirit is already present in your group, so your prayer is for group members—and you—to open hearts, minds, and souls to the presence of the Holy Spirit.

Here is one such prayer that you might use:

Almighty God, by and through your love you have surrounded us with your Holy Spirit. But we confess that often we do not open ourselves to the presence of your Spirit. Help us in this time of study to be open to and aware of your Spirit with us that our thoughts, words, and actions might enlighten, enable, and illuminate. We pray in the name of Christ Jesus. Amen.

Opening Activity

Distribute paper and pencils or pens. Ask each person in the group, working individually, to write on one side of the paper—for the writer's eyes only—the name of a person she or he needs to forgive and to describe briefly the reasons why this person needs to be forgiven. Also jot down at least one reason why forgiving this person is difficult.

Turn the paper over and write the name of a person whose forgiveness the writer wants and needs. Include a brief description of the reasons why the writer needs this person's forgiveness. Jot down why seeking this person's forgiveness is difficult.

Acknowledge that some group members may have to write the names of persons who may no longer be living or who may be unreachable for various reasons. Make it clear that these papers will not be distributed, discussed, or made known within the group in any way at any time.

When all have completed this assignment, suggest that group members fold their papers carefully and carry them in pocket, purse, or Bible for the duration of this study.

Learning Together

Video Study and Discussion
Play the video for Session 1.
Running time: 11:19

Forgiveness

Ask group members to form teams of three persons each and share quick definitions of forgiveness. Then ask the teams to think about and discuss this question: How is God's forgiveness of us like—and unlike—our forgiveness of one another?

Afterward, reconvene the large group and ask for brief reports from a few of the teams. Then discuss this question: Does forgiveness deal more with the past or the future? What is the immediate effect of forgiveness? What is the long-term result of forgiveness? Why do you answer as you do?

Sin

Can we understand forgiveness without a clear understanding of sin? Ask group members to define sin. Note that sin as described in the Bible is not so much individual acts or specific things we do or don't do, but missing the mark or straying from the path.

Pose this question for discussion by the whole group: What happens in life when we miss a mark or stray from a path and become lost? (Think in terms of shooting an arrow or trying to score in basketball.) Help group members recognize that when we miss a mark, we try to aim more accurately but sometimes overcompensate and miss the mark on the other side. Or, if we stray from a path and fear that we've become lost, our tendency might be to look for a shortcut and become even more lost. What do these life examples suggest about our response to sin?

Pose this question for brief discussion by the whole group: How does this definition of sin compare with your understanding of sin? Is this definition what we learned in Sunday school as children? Give examples and illustrations for your answers.

Repentance

Divide the group into pairs and discuss the meaning of repentance. Ask them to consider this question: What is the difference between contrition and repentance?

Afterward, ask for brief reports from several of the pairs. Help the group understand the difference between feeling sorry for our sinfulness (contrition) and turning around and getting back on the right path (repentance). What does this discussion say about experiencing God's forgiveness and experiencing forgiveness in our human relationships?

Book Study and Discussion

The Divine Answer

Theologian Paul Tillich describes forgiveness as the divine answer to the question implied in our existence. Tillich's statement suggests a single, basic question. Ask group members to suggest what that single question might be. Jot down responses for the group to consider, but do not evaluate these questions in detail yet. Keep the list of single questions for use in later sessions of this study.

Ego

"Healthy autonomy turns to unhealthy ego." Ask the group to consider the meaning of this sentence from Chapter 1. What is its biblical context? How does it apply to us? How can healthy autonomy coupled with an unhealthy ego create a widening gap between people, or between people and God? Must healthy autonomy always turn to unhealthy ego? How can we prevent that from happening in our own lives?

The Path

When we ask for or offer forgiveness, we are seeking restoration of a relationship that was severed through our sinfulness and failure to follow God's path. Discuss whether this is always the case. Does experiencing forgiveness—the forgiveness of God and of those we have wronged—always bring us back to the right path? Give reasons and illustrations for your answers.

Forgiveness as a Process

The process of forgiveness begins with our awareness of sin. A key word in this sentence is *process*. What does the use of this word say about forgiveness?

As a group, discuss some examples of Jesus forgiving sinners. How do these examples illustrate forgiveness as a process rather than as an instantaneous event? How might we experience that process, and how do we know when it is complete? How does failure to recognize that process impede the reestablishment of broken relationships with God and others?

Head or Heart?

Adam Hamilton writes that God's forgiveness "is something we know in our heads, and yet we often struggle to accept it in our hearts." In teams of three, discuss the differences between *understanding* the concept of forgiveness and *experiencing* actual forgiveness.

How can we move from understanding to experiencing? What factors might impede that movement? Encourage the teams to share personal examples of moving from "head" knowledge of forgiveness to "heart" experience of forgiveness. Do not ask for full reports from each team of three, but if a team is eager to share an insight, encourage that team to do so.

Bible Study and Discussion

Adam and Eve

Hamilton uses the story of Adam and Eve to illustrate sin as straying from the path or missing the mark. As a group, review the story and discuss: What caused Adam and Eve to stray from the path God had given them? Why were they not content with the limitations God had placed upon them? How could they have avoided this danger, and what can we learn from their experience?

In teams of four, discuss: What are the limitations God places upon us in our own lives, and why are we not content with those limitations? Hear very brief reports from a couple of the teams.

Wrapping Up

Closing Activity

To conclude the session, invite group members to look at the papers they wrote at the beginning of the session and to reflect on these questions silently: What have I learned today about the situation in which I need to forgive someone? What have I learned about the situation in which I need to seek forgiveness from another?

Closing Prayer

Close the session by inviting group members to recite the Lord's Prayer, pausing and meditating in silence when they reach this phrase: "Forgive us our trespasses as we forgive those who trespass against us." Then repeat the Lord's Prayer as a group again.

2.

For Better, for Worse

Getting Started

Session Goals

This session is intended to help participants

- Consider forgiveness in marriage and other intimate relationships;
- Gain new insights into the mutuality of relationships;
- Begin to recognize in their own relationships their propensity to "keep score" and seek justice rather than offering forgiveness;
- Identify and practice the building blocks of solid and lasting human relationships;
- Acknowledge and put into practice the role of grace and forgiveness in healthy and positive relationships.

Opening Prayer

Invite group members to join with you in the following prayer for others, based on words from John Calvin, a sixteenth-century

Protestant reformer in Switzerland and a contemporary of Martin Luther. You may want to write out this prayer on the board or duplicate it on handouts for group members.

> *Strong Covenant God, save us from being self-centered in our prayers, and teach us to remember to pray for others. May we be so bound up in love with those for whom we pray that we may feel their needs as acutely as our own, and intercede for them with sensitivity, understanding, and imagination. This we pray in Christ's name. Amen.*

Opening Activity

Divide your group into teams of four. Ask the teams to read 2 Samuel 11:1–12:9 and then discuss these questions:

What was David's sin in this story? About whose happiness was David most concerned? What happened as a result of David's eagerness to get his own way? Who among those in the story was most hurt by David's actions? As you respond to this last question, recall that David had several wives and a number of children prior to his relationship with Bathsheba.

Ask the teams to reflect on this statement: David's determination to meet his own desires escalated into sinfulness far beyond his original lust. In what ways does our lack of faithfulness in relationships escalate into our wandering farther and farther off the path that God has given us?

Reconvene and ask for brief reports from a few of the teams. Do most agree on responses to these questions? Why or why not?

Learning Together

Video Study and Discussion
Play the video for Session 2.
Running time: 12:35

"Accounting"

The author focuses on "accounting" in relationships. As a group, discuss: What is meant by this term? This same tendency is also called "keeping score." In this context, what does the phrase mean? Do we do this intentionally, or is it a subconscious habit? Where do you think this tendency comes from? Is it endemic in the human spirit, or is it something we have learned and developed through experience? Give reasons and illustrations for your responses.

What are some ways to counter this tendency? How can we do so in our marriages, friendships, work relationships, and extended families? How can we be sure we are not just offering one another verbal platitudes?

Forgiveness and Reconciliation

As a group, discuss: Is Christian forgiveness always possible? Is it always appropriate? And does Christian forgiveness always mean reconciliation? Give reasons and illustrations for your answers.

Six Words

Six words are crucial to making any relationship last and grow: "I am sorry" and "I forgive you." Write these words on the board, and consider them with reference to the following questions: Is saying these words enough to repair a torn relationship? Give reasons and illustrations for your answer. What else might be needed besides the words? Help the group members to recognize that what is being sought here is not the exchange of gifts or promises to be better in the future, but a genuineness in the offering of these words.

Book Study and Discussion

Medium-sized Stones

Ask group members to recall from the first chapter the metaphor of stones in a backpack. In a marriage or intimate relationship, what might constitute "medium-sized stones?" In other human relationships—with friends, family, and co-workers—what might constitute medium-sized stones? Discuss this metaphor. How is it useful? What are some of the things we can learn from it?

Justice

Divide the group into teams of four and discuss: Can seeking justice ever work in a relationship that has been harmed by medium-sized stones? Why or why not? Ask teams to define escalation and discuss how it relates to seeking justice in a relationship.

If time permits, ask the teams to try a simple role-play in which one person criticizes another team member through name-calling. Encourage the one who was called a name to respond with justice. Is the response equal to or harsher than the first? How might the person have responded differently?

Four Steps to Forgiveness

Review the four steps to forgiveness: awareness, regret, confession, and change. Then, divide the group into new teams of four and ask the teams to discuss: Which of these steps is the easiest to take? Which is the most difficult? Why do you think this is so? Which of the steps, if any, can be internal; and which can be shared with the one offended? Must these steps always be taken in the same order? Why or why not? Give illustrations, if possible.

Forgiveness in the Church

Suppose two leaders in your congregation disagree violently over some issue within the church, and suppose they have let the disagreement escalate until the congregation takes sides in the conflict. Discuss as a group: What can the rest of the congregation do to move the two leaders toward forgiveness? Who in the congregation should do this? How do you think the congregation's intervention would be received?

Bible Study and Discussion

Spiritual Garments

In Colossians 3:12, Paul writes, "Clothe yourselves with compassion, kindness, humility, meekness, and patience." Divide the group into teams of two to describe each of these qualities. Then, discuss which of the qualities is easiest to demonstrate and which is the most difficult. Why is this so? To what extent, if any, does demonstrating these qualities depend on the situation or circumstances of an experience?

Do not ask for reports from the teams, but if one or two of them wish to share a question or insight, invite them to do so.

Wrapping Up

Closing Activity

Invite group members to take out the papers they wrote at the last session (in which they named people to forgive and asked forgiveness of) and evaluate carefully both situations described. Ask group members to reflect in silence on the nature of the situations they have described. Are the situations pebbles, medium stones, or boulders? What insights into dealing with these situations have group members gained from this session? Do not ask for comments; encourage group members to reflect silently on these questions.

Closing Prayer

Invite group members to join you in the following sentence prayer. With the group repeat it aloud five times.

Lord Jesus Christ, teach me to forgive, and show me how to forgive as you forgive me.

19

3.

Seventy Times Seven

Getting Started

Session Goals

As a result of participation in this session, group members should

- consider forgiveness in relationships with those outside their families;
- identify and develop skills for dealing with everyday, petty annoyances;
- explore in some depth what forgiveness is—and what it is not;
- recognize the effects of forgiveness on the forgiver and the forgiven;
- begin to comprehend that merciful forgiveness may not always be the best course of action, and to develop skills in discerning those times when it is and is not appropriate;
- recognize and put into practice the teachings of Jesus dealing with forgiveness and reconciliation.

Opening Prayer

Invite group members to reflect on what they had written on their papers at the first session, then to pray in silence for insight and courage to do what needs to be done, in terms of both granting and seeking forgiveness. Next, invite the group to pray together the Lord's Prayer, pausing for silent reflection following each phrase in the prayer.

Opening Activity

Invite the whole group to participate in this activity; try if possible to make it light and fun.

Ask group members to call out petty annoyances while you jot these on the board. You might start with a question such as, "What just drives you up the wall?" If group members are slow to name things, suggest they focus on annoyances encountered while driving, dining out, standing in a checkout line, or watching TV. Try to develop a list at least twice as long as the number of members in your group. Keep this list in front of the group throughout this session.

Learning Together

Video Study and Discussion
Play the video for Session 3.
Running time: 10:02

Small Stones
Divide your group into teams of four, and ask the teams to discuss petty annoyances such as those posted on the board. How do you deal with these annoyances? How long do you remember a petty annoyance? Do you have to confront the person when it happens? How do you get over it? Have you ever had it ruin the next hour for you or the whole day? Let the members of each team share stories and illustrations.

RAP

Remind the group of the RAP process for dealing with petty annoyances: remember your own shortcomings, assume the best of people, and pray for them.

Do you think the RAP process will work? Can you think of cases when it won't? Why or why not? Which of the three steps would probably be hardest for you? Why?

Is Forgiving Enabling?

When Peter asked how many times he was to forgive, Jesus responded with an idiomatic phrase ("seventy times seven times") that meant, in essence, an infinite number of times. In pairs, discuss the following questions: Do you think we literally should forgive an infinite number of times? Should we always forgive the same person for the same offense? How do we know whether, in forgiving repeatedly, we are enabling bad behavior? Do we ever reach a point where we can legitimately say, "I've given you every possible chance and nothing has changed; no more forgiveness?"

Ask some of the pairs to report on their conversations and compare their conclusions.

Book Study and Discussion

In Your Own Words

Divide the group into four teams. Ask the members of each team to paraphrase—put into their own words—one or more of the author's significant statements. Then, give examples to illustrate.

Team 1: "Forgiveness means letting go of the right to redress or retribution."

Team 2: "If the aim of punishment is only retribution, then forgiveness may set aside the punishment. But if the aim of punishment is redemption, then the punishment may be essential. God works through consequences and punishment."

Team 3: "There is your internal release of bitterness, anger, or desire for revenge; and there is the extension of mercy toward the one who has wronged you."

Team 4: "Offering mercy before a person understands the need for it can diminish the gravity of the act."

Retribution or Redemption?

Ask the entire group to discuss two questions in some depth:

1. If punishment is deemed necessary in a situation, how can we be sure that the punishment we mete out is appropriate, redemptive, and positive, rather than vindictive? Is it always our place to mete out punishment? Give examples and illustrations for answering as you do.

2. If extending mercy too early in the process can be inappropriate, how do we know the best time to extend mercy? How do we know if the offender truly understands the need for mercy and forgiveness? Again, give examples and illustrations.

A Biblical Process for Reconciliation

Form your group into two teams and give them this assignment: Skim over the section titled "A Biblical Process for Reconciliation," then develop a brief role-play in which a church member has been deeply hurt by another member. What does the offended church member do? To whom does the member report this offense? How should it be reported? Continue in the role-play as if the offender still refuses to recognize the offense. What are the next steps? Act out the process, with the rest of the team playing the part of the church.

Reconvene and discuss: Does the process described by Jesus work in our day and age? Why or why not? Do we use this process in our time? Should we? Why or why not? How should the two members and the church deal with counterclaims in these situations—that is, when both people feel they are the offended party? What is the role of the church in such a situation?

Bible Study and Discussion

The Really Big Stone

What is the greatest sin in the Bible, the really big stone? Divide the group into teams of four, and ask the teams to read Matthew 26:14-16 and Matthew 27:3-10. Then ask them, as a team, to discuss:

Why did the chief priests agree to the betrayal of Jesus? Was their sin greater or less than the sin of Judas? Give reasons for your answer.

Describe what you believe took place in Judas's mind and heart after the Crucifixion. How does his action reflect (or not reflect) the four basic components of repentance described in the book (awareness, regret, confession, and change)? What was Judas trying to do when he attempted to return the thirty pieces of silver?

Why did Judas hang himself? If Judas had seen Jesus after the Resurrection, what do you think would have been Jesus' response to Judas? Would the mercy of Jesus have waived the consequences of Judas' act? In other words, even though Christ may have forgiven Judas, would Judas still have hanged himself? Give reasons for your answers.

Hear brief reports from a couple of the teams.

Wrapping Up

Closing Prayer

Ask group members to look again at the petty annoyances you listed on the board at the beginning of this session. Invite them to pray in silence for those in their lives who are guilty of petty annoyances; those who are guilty of medium-sized stones; and those who have inflicted great pain and suffering.

When all have prayed in silence, ask the group to recognize prayerfully the ways in which they are guilty of petty annoyances, of inflicting mid-sized stones, and of causing great suffering for others. Remind them that awareness of our own shortcomings is the crucial first step toward repentance and wholeness.

Then ask group members to repeat these lines of prayer after you:

Lord Jesus Christ,
Son of God,
Savior of the world:
Have mercy on us. Amen.

Encourage group members to make this their breath prayer for the week.

4.

The Dreamcoat

Getting Started

Session Goals

As a result of participating in this session, group members should be able to

- reflect constructively and creatively on forgiveness in families;
- recognize and acknowledge the lasting impact of family relationships, both positive and negative;
- realize aspects of their families of origin that still affect them;
- develop skills in dealing with stones and walls constructed within their families of origin and their present families;
- carefully and prayerfully evaluate their own conduct and the effect it has on the members of the families in which they now live;
- learn to forgive in the context of family.

Opening Prayer

Invite group members to join you in the following prayer. You may want to post the prayer on the board or make copies to distribute.

Almighty and loving God: You have placed us within families, and we acknowledge that our families are the source of both our greatest joys and our deepest hurts and pains.

We often find that forgiving outsiders is so much easier than forgiving those within our families. We often find that hurting family members is so much easier than hurting outsiders.

We often save our best behavior for settings outside our homes and show our worst selves to our own families.

Lord God, we need you to help us love our family members when they are most unlovable, just as you love us when we are most unlovable.

Above and beyond it all, Lord, we thank you for our families. We ask you to bless them and to make us blessings within our families.

We pray all this in the name of Christ Jesus. Amen.

Opening Activity

Pass out paper and pens or pencils. Ask the group to jot quick answers to the following questions that you will read aloud. What group members write is for their eyes only; these responses will not be shared in any way.

Who in your family of origin brought you the most joy?
Who brought you the most pain and suffering?

27

Of whom in your family were you most jealous?
Who did you most want to be like?

Now think about your current family or group of friends. List three areas of needed improvement in that group. What are you doing now to improve those relationships?

These papers are for the writers' eyes only. Suggest that group members look back at what they have written following this session, then a few days later.

Learning Together

Video Study and Discussion
Play the video for Session 4.
Running time: 11:47

Wounds and Scars
Physical wounds often leave scars long after healing has taken place, and these scars remind us of the physical wounds. Do the wounds caused by relationships also leave scars after the healing takes place? What kinds of scars? Just as we might use makeup to cover a physical scar, what do we use to cover up an emotional scar? Explain your answers with illustrations from books and movies (or from your own lives).
Then discuss: Does forgiveness remove the scars? Does reconciliation remove the scars? Give reasons for your answers.

Book Study and Discussion

Stones in Families
In the large group, discuss ways in which family members can deal with boulders or even mid-sized stones. How can one confront a family member in a loving, forgiving way? What are some ways in which prayer can help, for both the offender and the

victim? What kinds of questions and issues sometimes remain unresolved? Explain your answers.

Dealing with Confrontation

Confrontation is one possible response to family problems. Suggest ways of reacting to comments from the offender such as "You're being too sensitive," "I was only kidding," "That was nothing compared with what you've done to me," or "Let's just pretend it never happened."

Discuss: Are any of these responses legitimate? How can the offended party tell if he or she is being too sensitive? Can the offended family member simply pretend the hurt never took place? Why or why not?

The Cross

Form three teams from your group members, and then read aloud the following passage from Adam Hamilton's book:

> The cross teaches us that God can take the pain and suffering of our past and, when we put them in his hands, produce something beautiful. That is why some have defined forgiveness as giving up the hope of a different past. . . . Forgiveness is believing that the future can be better than the past.

Ask the teams to paraphrase the passage. Compare the paraphrases from the three teams, and discuss the differences.

Bible Study and Discussion

Abraham and Isaac

As a whole group, outline the stories of Abraham, Isaac, and Jacob on the newsprint or chalkboard. Let group members call out events in the lives of these patriarchs and try to get them in biblical and chronological order. You might suggest that group members identify those events in these stories that were positive influences on the family and those that were basically negative. Here's a hint: Abraham's willingness to let his nephew have the choice of land was a positive influence; Abraham's attemp—twice! —to pass off his wife as his sister was a negative, even though this may have been the culture of the time.

What other incidents in Abraham's life could be viewed as stones of various sizes for the family members? The author cites Abraham's favoritism of Isaac over Ishmael as a negative, but what was the source of this incident? Who played significant roles in this event? Whose feelings were hurt by this event, and how were they hurt? (If the group members stumble a bit here, refer them to Genesis 21:8-21)

How about the sacrifice of Isaac in Genesis 22? Do group members believe that Sarah was a party to this? Did she protest when Abraham announced he was to sacrifice their son? Did Abraham even tell Sarah where he and Isaac were going that fateful day?

Move on to Isaac, again recognizing incidents that were positive for the family and those that were negative. What might be the short-term and the long-term effect of parental favoritism, especially if wife and husband favor different sons?

Joseph

Review the story of Joseph and the dreamcoat. Sibling rivalry, mendacity of the highest order, long-term fear and distrust—this story is full of family issues.

What insights into the ways in which God works can be gained from this litany of lying, cheating, threatening, blackmail, betrayal, and all the rest? If group members seem to falter here, ask them to complete this sentence: "If God could use people from such dysfunctional families as Joseph's, then surely God can. . . "

Wrapping Up

Closing Prayer

Invite group members to look again at the papers they wrote at the first session describing one person they want to forgive and one person whose forgiveness they need. Offer a silent prayer for God's guidance in these tasks. Then, ask members to prepare an action plan for each.

Afterward, invite group members to offer aloud sentence prayers of thanks for the forgiveness Christ provides and for the courage to offer and receive the forgiveness from others.

Epilogue

1. In Genesis 1, we read that humans are made in the "image of God." What does that mean to you? In what ways is it easy to believe? In what ways is it difficult to believe?

2. In discussing ways in which we fall short of God's image, Adam Hamilton cites the examples of Adam and Eve, Cain and Abel, and Lamech. What other examples would you cite from the Bible? from today's world? from your own life?

3. Hamilton also cites examples of ways in which we live up to God's image, including the stories of Victoria Ruvolo, Jesus' follower Stephen, and Reginald and Margaret Green. What other examples would you cite from the Bible? What examples would you cite from today's world and your own life?

4. With these examples in mind of actions that show or don't show people living up to the image of God, what further thoughts and conclusions do you have about the *imago Dei?*

5. Hamilton writes, "If there's someone in your life you long to forgive, or whose forgiveness you seek, don't wait." Why does he offer this advice? How does it make you feel?

6. Take a few minutes to think about and perhaps write down the name of one person in your own life whose forgiveness you long for; and the name of one person you long to forgive. Imagine what you might tell these people, and when. Write down how you would feel if you lost the chance to tell them.

7. Ponder together the ultimate act of forgiveness: Jesus' words and actions on the cross. What do you think they mean? What difference could they make in your life?